When Gymnasts Made History

A photographic celebration of the achievements
of Britain's artistic gymnasts
at the
London 2012 Olympic Games

by Eileen Langsley

The text and all images are by Eileen Langsley.
Quotes are copyright of the person attributed.
Eileen Langsley asserts the moral rights to be identified as the author of this work. All rights reserved.
No part of this publication may be reproduced, stored in a retrieval system, scanned or transmitted by any means
electronic, mechanical, photo copying, recording or otherwise without the prior written permission
of Eileen Langsley.

Copyright © Eileen Langsley 2013. Published by EGB Books UK.
First published January 2013.

http://www.langsleysports.com

© Eileen Langsley 2013

Eileen Langsley retains sole copyright to her contributions to this book.
Any attributed text is the copyright of the author.

www.langsleysports.com

Published by EGB Books UK

ISBN
978-0-9572370-4-9

To Steve + Del
I hope this keeps the memories alive.
Love,
Eileen
January 2013

The Blurb-provided layout designs and graphic elements are copyright Blurb Inc., 2012.

Contents

A series of themed photographic essays with quotes and comments.

1. Let The Games Begin!
2. Ready To Go - The Gymnasts in Training.
3. The Qualification Competitions.
4. The Team Finals.
5. The All Around Finals.
6. The Apparatus Finals.
7. The Emotional Games.
8. In Praise Of Coaches.
9. These Too Made The Games.
10. A Personal Olympics.
11. The Enduring Games.
12. Acknowledgements.

Let The Games Begin!

"Competing in an Olympic Games is special anyway but competing in one in your own country is amazing."
Nicky Richards

When Gymnasts Made History

"To the athletes, gathered here on the eve of this great endeavor, I say that to you is given something precious and irreplaceable. To run faster, to jump higher, to be stronger. I offer this thought: your talent, dedication and commitment brought you here. Now you have a chance to become true Olympians. That honour is determined not by whether you win, but by how you compete. Character counts far more than medals."
Jacques Rogge President of the IOC

"To all the Olympians who came to London to compete - thank you. Those of us who came to watch, witnessed moments of heroism and heartbreak that will live long in the memory. You have our admiration and our congratulations."
Lord Sebastian Coe

When Gymnasts Made History

When Gymnasts Made History

Ready To Go

"The team has great belief that through their reliance and responsibility to one another, their efforts will be rewarded."
Eddie Van Hoof

"It is such a warm feeling to have the Olympics in London. There is a lot of pressure on me to do well but I will try to deal with it in a way that a professional athlete would. It's been an emotional four years. There's been a lot of pressure on my shoulders, a lot of people have put a lot of hours into supporting me."
Louis Smith

"I'll keep doing my job; I'm looking for a top ten finish and hopefully a medal. That's my goal."
Daniel Purvis

Max Whitlock, and Louis Smith (facing page) and Daniel Purvis (this page) during official podium training at the London 2012 Olympic Games.

When Gymnasts Made History

"Everyone is working on some really big goals together as a unit, which also means we can all support each other."
Hannah Whelan

When Gymnasts Made History

Hannah Whelan (facing page) and Jenni Pinches (this page) during official podium training at the London 2012 Olympic Games.

When Gymnasts Made History

Max Whitlock during training

When Gymnasts Made History

Sam Oldham during training

"No stone was left unturned. The team had great depth and experience including three past Olympians and the current British Champion. Absolute key was the support staff of coaches and EIS personnel."
Colin Still

When Gymnasts Made History

British coaches during training at the London 2012 Olympic Games:- Amanda Reddin, Colin Still and Eddie Van Hoof (facing page), Andrei Popov and Paul Hall (this page).

When Gymnasts Made History

"She's the only gymnast I've ever worked with that's given 100 per cent day in day out and I'm very proud she walked through my door all those years ago."
Amanda Reddin

When Gymnasts Made History

Under the watchful eye of her coach Amanda Reddin, Beth Tweddle trains before the Apparatus Finals.

When Gymnasts Made History

When Gymnasts Made History

"I worked really hard to get here. But we've got a big job to do."
Max Whitlock

Max Whitlock, Kristian Thomas, Sam Oldham, (facing page) and Daniel Purvis and Louis Smith (this page) during official podium training at the London 2012 Olympic Games.

"It's been worth it.
This is the best experience of my life.
Not many people can say they've been to an Olympics at the age of 15 so it is an achievement."
Rebecca Tunney

When Gymnasts Made History

Imogen Cairns, Rebecca Tunney, Hannah Whelan (facing page) and Beth Tweddle (this page) during official podium training at the London 2012 Olympic Games.

The Qualification Competitions

Rebecca Tunney (this page), Hannah Whelan, Jenni Pinches, Imogen Cairns (facing page), competing and celebrating during the qualification competition at the London 2012 Olympic Games.

"The qualification competition is crucial because it doesn't matter what you do if you don't get through to the final".

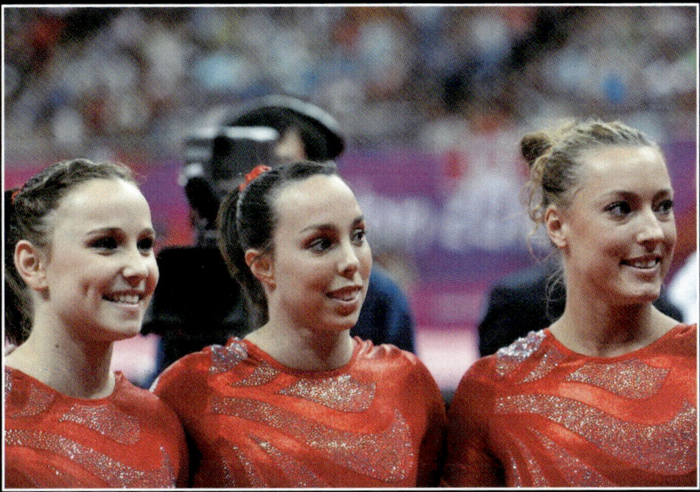

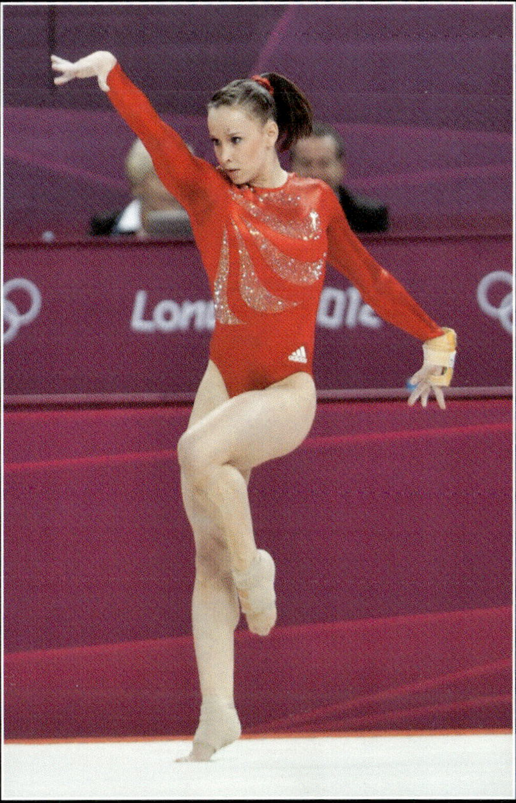

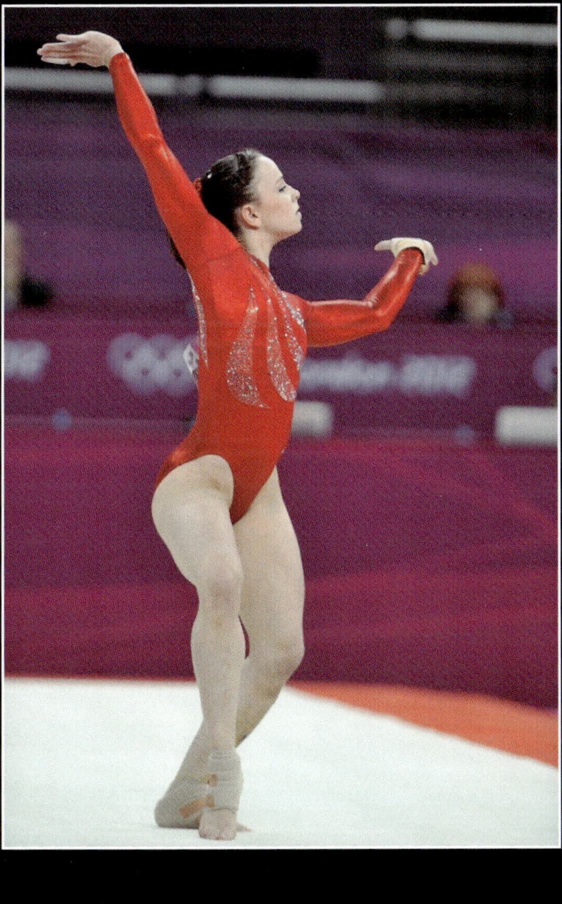

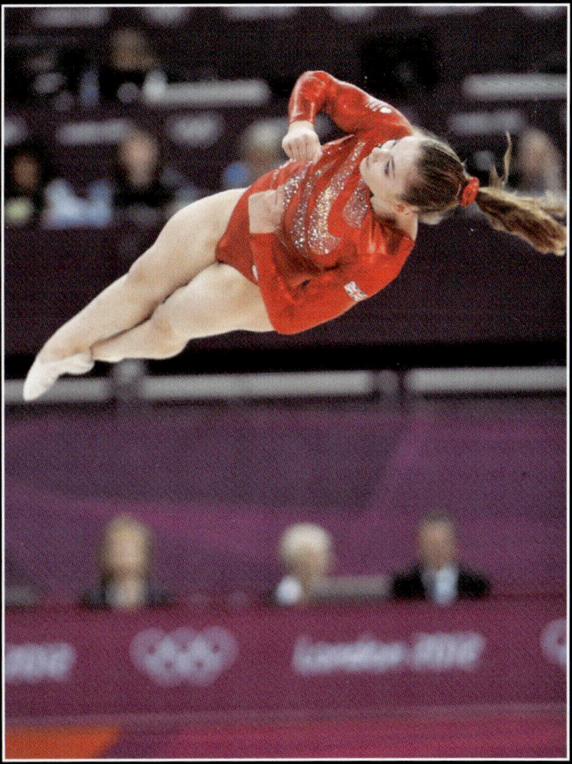
London 2012

Max Whitlock (this page) and Daniel Purvis, Sam Oldham,
Louis Smith and Kristian Thomas (facing page) during the
qualifications competition at the London 2012 Olympic Games.

25

When Gymnasts Made History

"The very last performance was Beth's bars and that gave the team their first team qualification final ever and Beth her qualification for Bars final."
Christine Still

Both Pages - Beth Tweddle qualifies for the Asymmetric Bars Final with an outstanding performance.

"I've thought about this competition and this bars routine for so long and to produce my best score this Olympic cycle in qualifying - it couldn't be any better. I spoke to Louis Smith about the crowd and pressure and what to expect and he said they lifted him and it was definitely the same for me today, the atmosphere was incredible. Today was the big pressure day, people tried to calm me but deep down you know you have to perform so to go out and do it is brilliant. "

Beth Tweddle

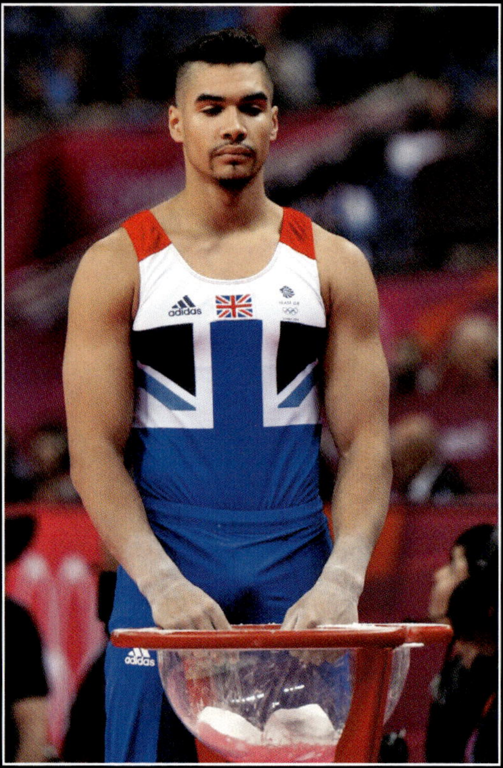
adidas

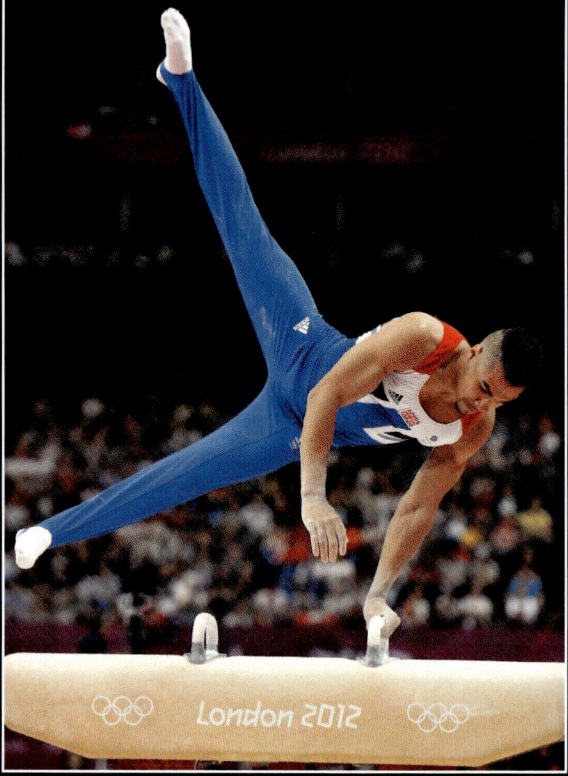
London 2012

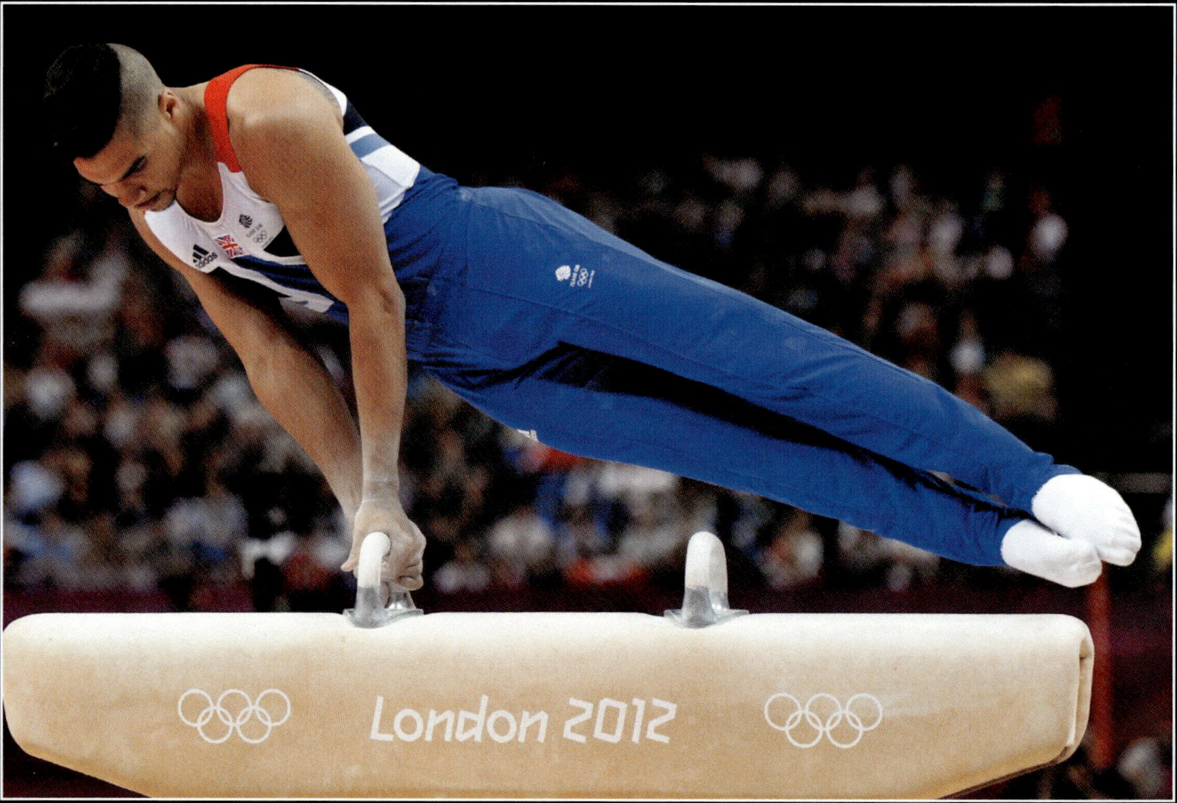
adidas
London 2012

"The team spirit is really good, especially seeing Louis in tears at the end. You don't really expect that from Louis, he's a cool guy. I was just hoping it was tears of happiness on his great score."
Daniel Purvis

Both pages - An emotional Louis Smith produces a great routine to qualify for the Pommel Horse Final.

"The team are like sisters and we all pulled together today and relished the pressure. The balance of the team with the experience of Imogen Cairns going up first on beam and Rebecca Tunney only 15 and performing brilliantly - and Hannah and Jenni with great all-around displays - it worked perfectly. The gymnasts have done a great job both days for GB,."

"China are the world champions, they are awesome and I really think they'll pull it up a level on Monday in the team final."
Daniel Purvis

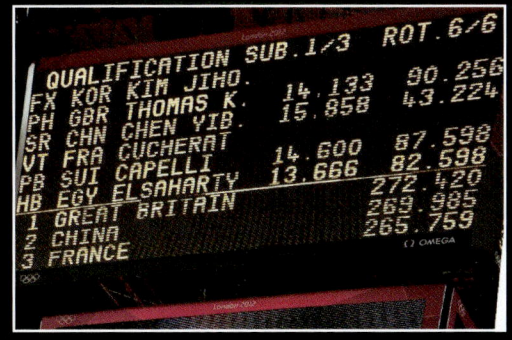

"Beating the Chinese is unbelievable. One of the things we always say is not to worry about the others, we know what we're capable of. Beating them is a pat on the back for us, we've had a long journey to get here. We're on new ground now. We've not qualified a team before so I think we've already exceeded expectations and we're just going to enjoy it."
Louis Smith

The Team Finals

After making history in the Qualification Competitions, the British gymnasts and coaches face up to the challenge of the Team Finals.

When Gymnasts Made History

A confident performance on the asymmetric bars from Rebecca Tunney, Hannah Whelan and Beth Tweddle during the Women's Team Final at the London 2012 Olympic Games.

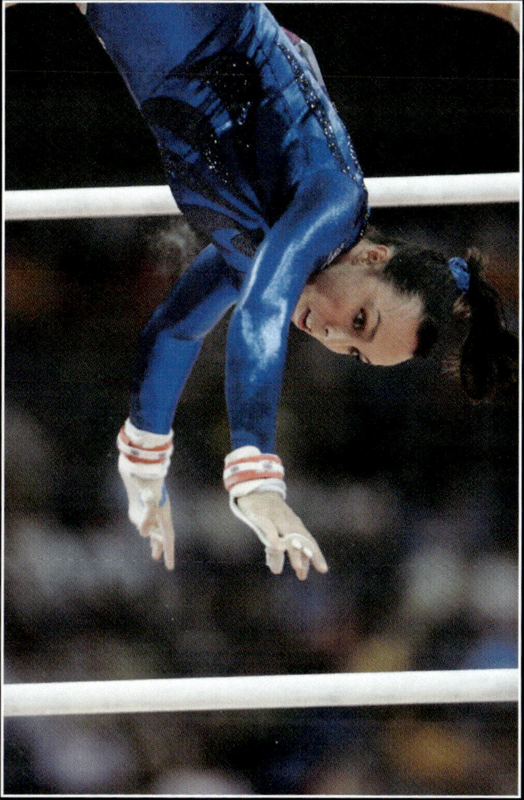
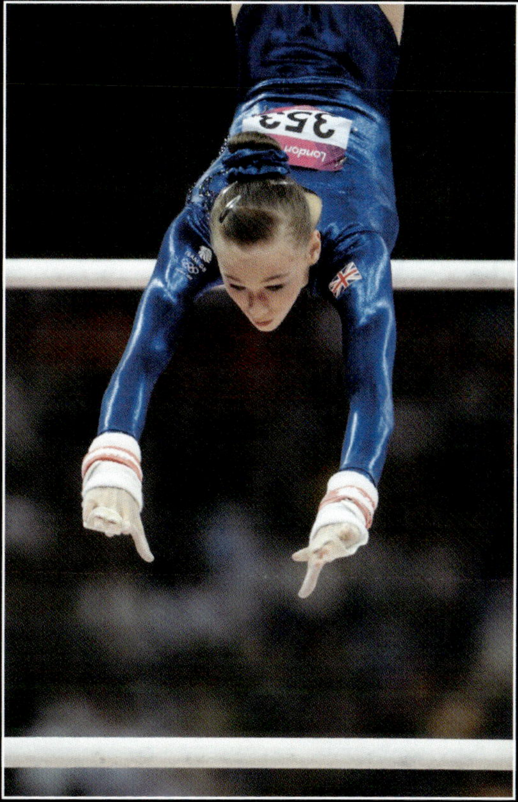
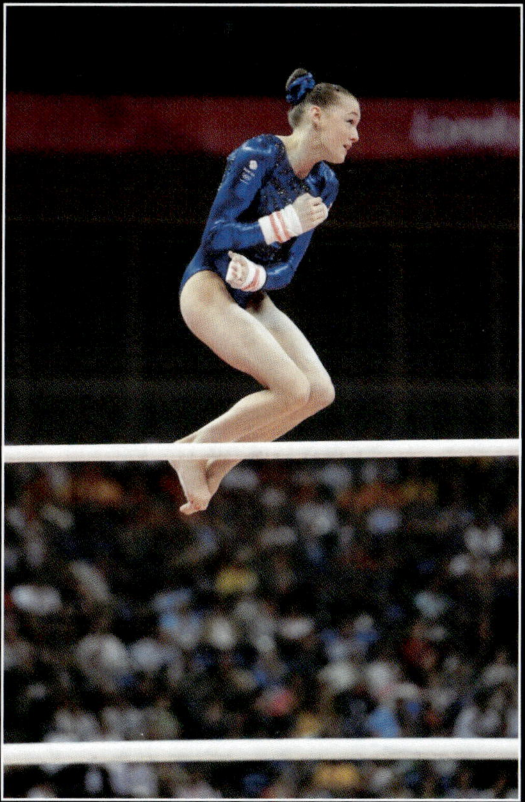
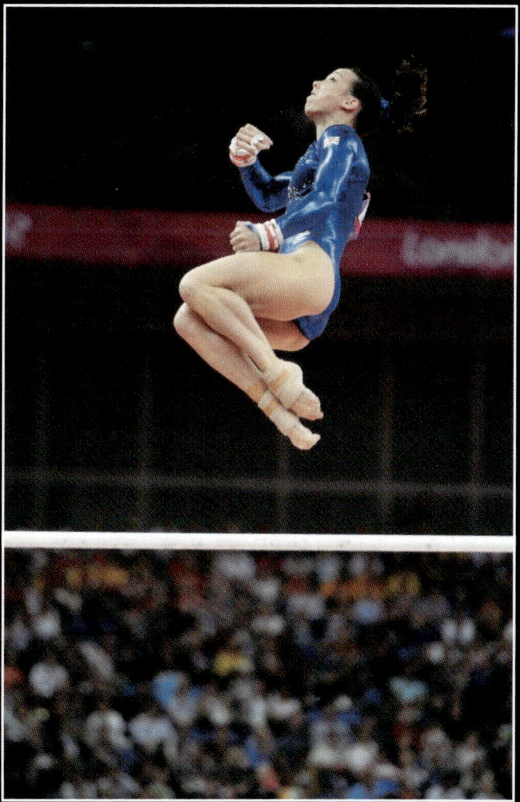

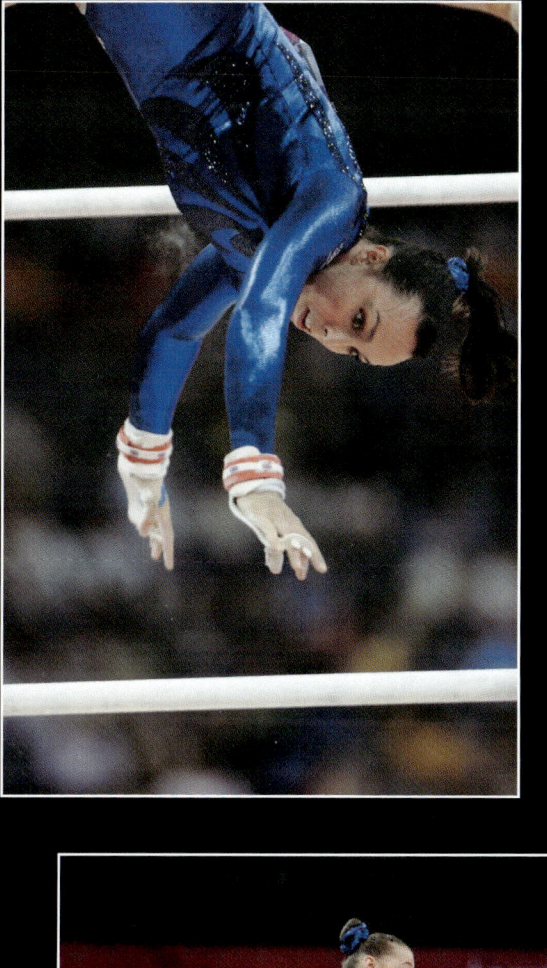

Making a confident start on Pommel Horse and Rings - Daniel Purvis, Louis Smith and Max Whitlock (this page) Kristian Thomas, Sam Oldham and Damiel Purvis (facing page).

37

When Gymnasts Made History

"My team-mates have done me proud today. We've gone out there in front of a home crowd and we've finished sixth in the world. Four years ago we didn't even make the team final."
Beth Tweddle

"It was an amazing achievement for the men. We were never going to go out today to try and replicate that or do better than them. It wasn't about being against them. We're moving up and up so it's all good."
Hannah Whelan

Emotional scenes as the British Women's Team celebrate their historic sixth place finish in the Team Final.

When Gymnasts Made History

40

Maintaining the challenge on High Bar - Daniel Purvis, Sam Oldham, and Kristian Thomas.

"I tried not to look at the scores all the way round, as it was so close but I couldn't resist after High Bar. The crowd were incredible and really helped us through."
Kristian Thomas

"This was pure theatre. I was there in the crowd and was amazed by the way the British guys performed, particularly Kristian Thomas with that high-flying floor routine. The fact that Britain were awarded the silver only to be dropped back down to bronze just added to the drama."

Lord Sebastian Coe

"We came out and we delivered. We showed the world what we're capable of. We all have smiles on our faces -
it's monstrous."
Louis Smith

"It's been a long old journey to get here. It was tough a few years ago, and where we've come from, to come here, the pinnacle of our sport, being a GB athlete at the London Olympics, to do that was just amazing."
Louis Smith

When Gymnasts Made History

MEN'S TEAM FINAL
VICTORY CEREMONY
GOLD   CHINA
SILVER JAPAN
BRONZE GREAT BRITAIN

London 2012

"With only a slight setback in the Japan World Championships of 2011 the GB men's team have demonstrated the most spectacular and consistent progress year on year winning Olympic Team Bronze in London 2012 with a bonus of pommel horse Silver and Bronze. This was achieved by bringing together a remarkable talent pool of gymnasts, coaches and clubs to work into a single system and programme driven by the National Governing Body and funded by Sport UK. The unwavering support and solidarity of the partnership was always going to result in success; the gymnasts and the coaches now stand as equals amongst the greatest in the world."

Trevor Low

"We thought we had the silver but the colour doesn't matter ... I am standing here with an Olympic medal and I can't stop looking at it."
Kristian Thomas

"Our results over the past few years seem to have got better and better and we are starting to get more recognition from the outside world. We can also show the world that we are a force to be reckoned with."

Kristian Thomas

When Gymnasts Made History

Kristian Thomas turns in a fine performance for a seventh place finish in the All Around Finals of the London 2012 Olympic Games.

When Gymnasts Made History

Hannah Whelan and Rebecca Tunney competing in the All Around Finals of the London 2012 Olympic Games.

When Gymnasts Made History

"It's been an amazing experience here in London; the best week of my life. To compete at a home Games in front of this crowd has been incredible. To be the youngest in Team GB I'm very proud and I've learnt so much. I'm looking forward to the rest of the Games."
Rebecca Tunney

49

Supported throughout by coach Andrei Popov, Daniel Purvis finishes in 13th place in the All Around Finals at the London 2012 Olympic Games.

When Gymnasts Made History

"At the Olympics the crowd really was like having an extra team member, encouraging us when things didn't go to plan and cheering us when things went well."
Kristian Thomas

The historic results of London 2012 were further enhanced in the Apparatus Finals when Kristian Thomas, Max Whitlock, Louis Smith and Beth Tweddle qualified to compete in Vault, Pommel Horse and Asymmetric Bars Finals respectively.

"I didn't even think I would get a medal, so it's an amazing feeling. I just wanted to go out there and do a clean routine. It was basically whoever did the cleanest routine would get a medal and Louis did a great job and I'm really happy to get a medal. I have two bronze medals now so this is unbelievable. It's crazy."

Max Whitlock

Beth Tweddle wins the bronze medal on Asymmetric Bars becoming the first British woman to win an Olympic medal in an individual gymnastics competition.

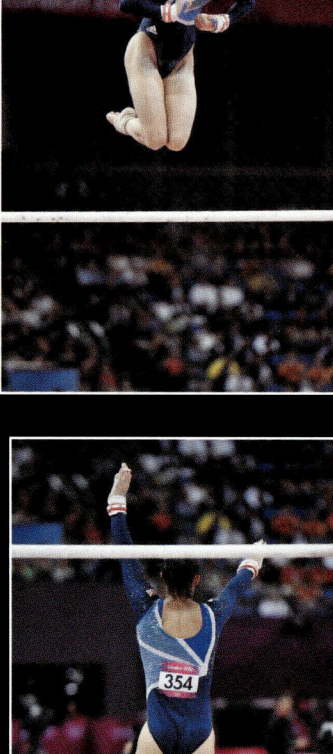

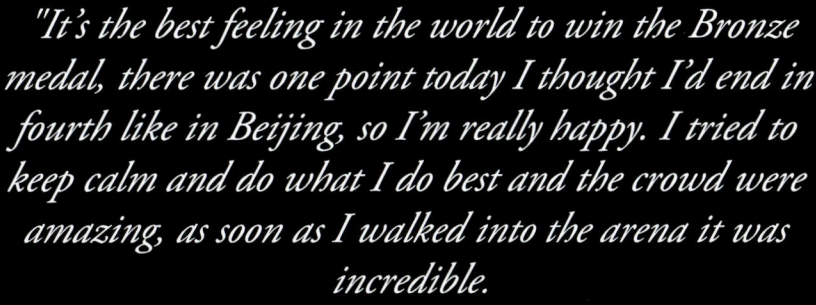

When Gymnasts Made History

"It's the best feeling in the world to win the Bronze medal, there was one point today I thought I'd end in fourth like in Beijing, so I'm really happy. I tried to keep calm and do what I do best and the crowd were amazing, as soon as I walked into the arena it was incredible.
I had a step on my dismount but at the end of the day I had to go for the difficult dismount to challenge for a medal. To be honest I could say 'what if?' but I'm not disappointed in the slightest, any medal, any colour is what I always said I wanted, so I'm extremely happy. Everyone knows this is the one medal that was missing from my collection, and this is the one I wanted. Amanda was just saying to me, 'Calm down, do what you do in the gym, it doesn't matter what happens today.' I won't be looking back. Before these Games I said any medal, any colour, I'll be happy, and I'm going to stick to that."
Beth Tweddle

"It's been a long four years for Beth, it's all she's wanted and I'm really happy for her."
Amanda Reddin

55

When Gymnasts Made History

"I wasn't too focused on what anyone else was doing. My routine was hard enough, let alone trying to worry about what anyone else was trying to do. So I just tried to stay focused, stay chilled, listen to my music and keep calm. Krisztian Berki will go down as one of the greatest pommel horse workers ever, and the fact that I came second to him is something I'm proud of. We're good friends. We are great rivals, but we are good friends. If I was going to be beaten by anyone apart from Max, then Krisztian Berki is that guy."

Louis Smith

Relief and pleasure as Louis Smith wins the silver medal in the Pommel Horse Final.

When Gymnasts Made History

Celebrating success - gymnasts Max Whitlock, Louis Smith and Beth Tweddle with coaches Eddie Van Hoof, Amanda Reddin and Paul Hall.

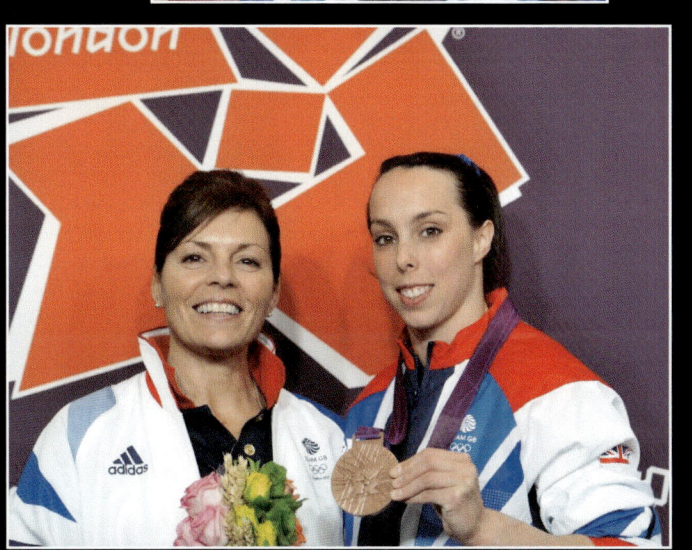

"The way Louis and Beth handled pressure to win medals for the home team with class and dignity, they showed beautifully how to win the silver and bronze medals rather than lose the gold."

Paul Ziert - International Gymnast

The Emotional Games

The roller coaster of emotions experienced by the British Women's Team and coach Amanda Reddin.

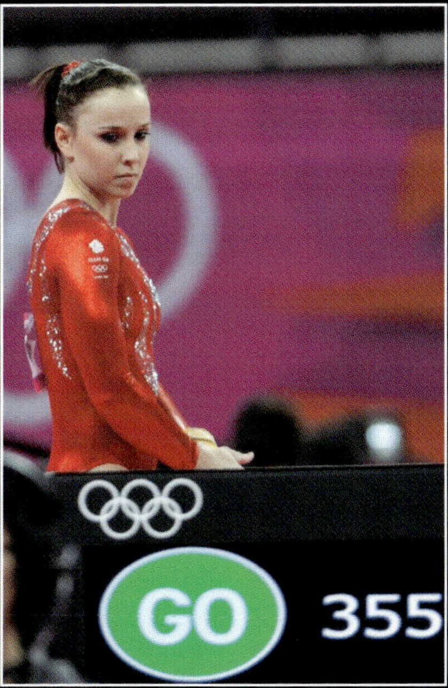
GO
355
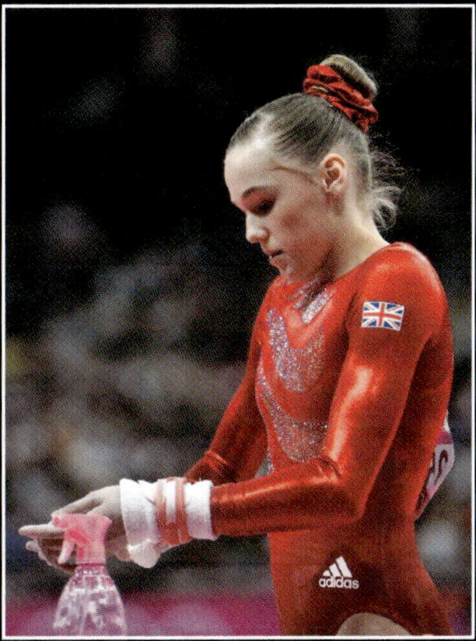
adidas
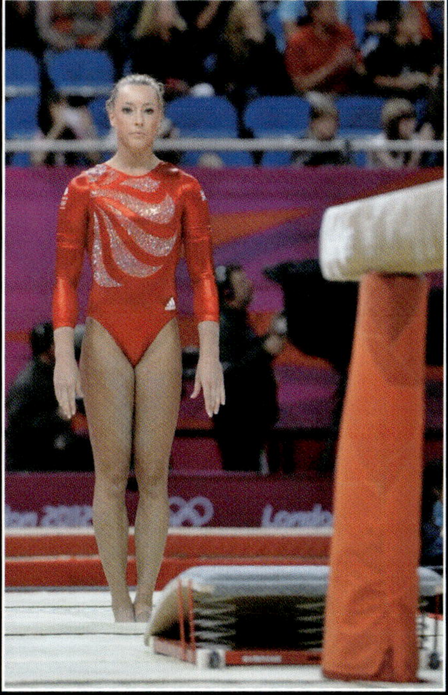
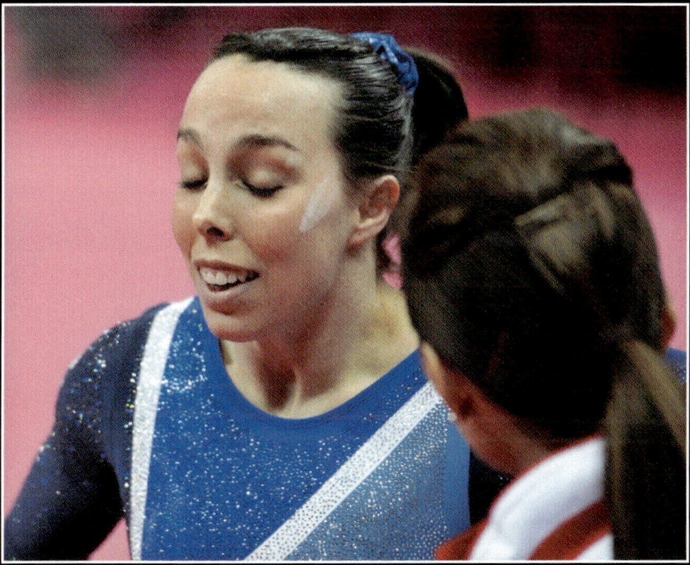
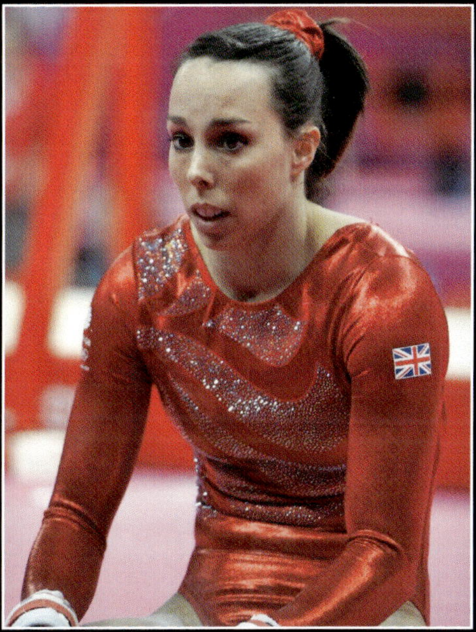
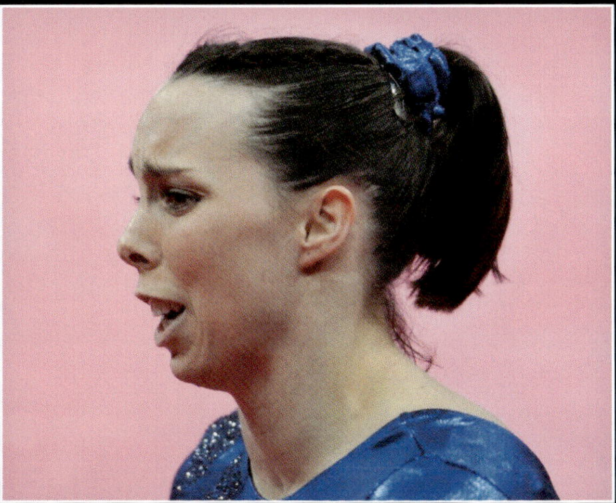
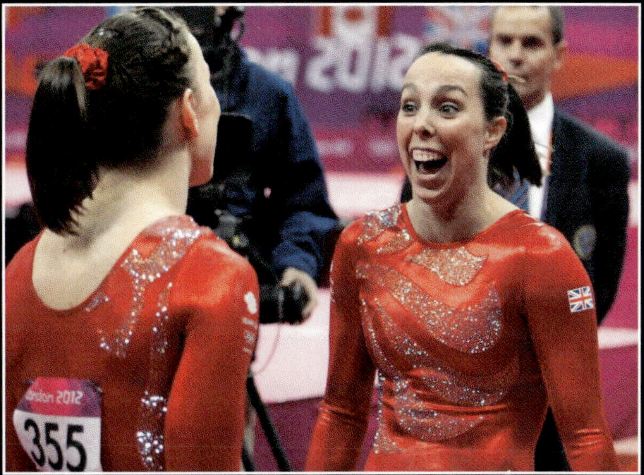
355

When Gymnasts Made History

Anxious moments combine with relief as the British Men's Team win their historic bronze medal in the Team Competition.

When Gymnasts Made History

"This is a dream come true for all of us. For these guys, it's their first Olympics, so to get a medal, a bronze medal, is unbelievable."

Louis Smith

London 2012

63

Louis Smith and coaches Paul Hall and Eddie Van Hoof experience the agony and the ecstasy in the quest for Olympic glory.

When Gymnasts Made History

"It's unbelievable, really. It's been an emotional four years for the whole of British Gymnastics, there has been a lot of pressure to perform at these Olympics since Beijing. I've never experienced anything quite like it. It's the best feeling in the world."
Louis Smith

65

In Praise of Coaches

"As a coach you don't only want to produce and inspire good gymnasts, you want to inspire generations of coaches to come."
Christine Still

"I'm very proud of what Amanda has achieved. She has been the backbone of British Gymnastics for the past few years."
Christine Still

Coaches Amanda Reddin and Colin Still along with team physiotherapist Louise Fawcett, support and encourage the British Women's Team.

When Gymnasts Made History

"'In this story it is not a coincidence that the team who qualified for Barcelona in 1992 and the team who won Olympic Bronze in 2012 were both led by Eddie Van Hoof. A great team, a superb partnership and inspired leadership."
Trevor Low

When Gymnasts Made History

Eddie Van Hoof gives support and advice to the team in training and competition at the London 2012 Olympic Games.

69

When Gymnasts Made History

Supporting, advising, waiting, watching and celebrating - coaches Andrei Popov and Paul Hall along with team physiotherapist Alastair Little at the London 2012 Olympic Games.

When Gymnasts Made History

Paul Hall sees his many years of work come to fruition.

71

"It's important we recognise those people who have given so much to the sport in the past, not only staff but also the volunteers who for years have been the backbone of the sport."

Matthew Greenwood

When Gymnasts Made History

Years of inspired leadership. hard work and superb organisation behind the scenes ensured a truly great Olympic Games.

"Feeling the massive support from the British public has been like a dream."
Rebecca Tunney

"That was just unbelievable. The support we have had is remarkable…it adds pressure and expectation but you can use that to your advantage."
Louis Smith

With success comes the pressure of being the focus of media attention.

A Personal Olympics

Having previously been present at a number of Olympic Games, London 2012 held particular significance for me as it would be my thirteenth experience of what can only be described as the greatest sporting event on the planet. It has been a huge privilege for me to witness some of the greatest moments in the history of sport and as a photographer, to be a part of the media that has spread the Olympic message around the world.

It was with a wry smile that I enjoyed a whimsical moment during the pre Games training sessions at the Gymnastics venue when I realised that I had, in my time, photographed most of the British and overseas coaches in the arena, when they themselves were gymnasts competing in World and Olympic events. I have been fortunate to witness the sport of Gymnastics grow and develop throughout the world and nowhere more so than in Great Britain. For us, the past had seen exceptional gymnasts such as Nik Stuart and Neil Thomas take their place on the world stage but gradually Britain began to show the talent and potential that promised more.

Slowly and carefully, the essential training system was put in place, talented coaches developed and essential funding was provided by UK Sport and the National Lottery. A superb national training facility was built at Lilleshall and the results started to happen. British born and overseas coaches helped gymnasts achieve their potential and for a select few, realise their Olympic dreams. Great Britain is now seen as a major player on the world stage and a force to be reckoned with. London 2012 could have provided no better stage for the world to bear witness to the results of this phenomenal work and progress.

When Gymnasts Made History

The Olympic Games stand for all that is inspirational in the world of sport and for encouraging and supporting all those qualities we hope to develop in our young people. May the lighting of the Olympic Torch in London 2012 be a true beacon for the future – one that will inspire generations to come.

Eileen Langsley

The Enduring Games

*"Today sees the closing of a wonderful Games in a wonderful city.
We lit the flame and lit up the world.
Finally, there are some famous words you can find stamped on the bottom of a product.
Words that, when you read them, you know mean high quality, mean skill, mean creativity.
We've stamped those words on the
Olympic and Paralympic Games
of London 2012.*

LONDON 2012 – 'MADE IN BRITAIN'. "

Lord Sebastian Coe

"There is no better feeling than representing your country at the Olympic Games."
Daniel Purvis

Acknowledgements

"London was a world wide success hailed by everyone affiliated to it. The Games of the XXX Olympiad in London were a foretaste of what perfection could look like."
Bruno Grandi

My thanks to all whose words have enhanced the images in this book and as ever, my gratitude to the gymnasts, coaches, support staff, organisers, officials and Games Makers who have been such an inspiration.
Eileen Langsley

Published by EGB Books UK
First published January 2013
www.langsleysports.com

ISBN

978-0-9572370-4-9

blurb